This prayer jourer
parents, grandpare
loved ones who have and are going on this journey with
them and have shown love and support through prayer. To
the Airmen and Vets thank you for your service. We hope
that this prayer journal is helpful and serves as a guide
during times of first good-byes, training, deployments,
and the everyday sacrifice that our Airmen and families
endure by keeping our country safe.
God Bless you all.

Be•Inspired
A subsidiary of:
Two Girls and a Reading Corner
© 2021 Mandy Leigh
ISBN: 978-1-952879-27-2

All rights reserved. No part of this book may be reproduced in any form without written permission from the publisher.
Designed © 2021 by
Mandy Leigh and Van Andrews

Two Girls and a Reading Corner
PO Box 2404, Madison, Al 35758

United States Air Force Prayer

Lord guard and guide the men
and women who fly,
Through the great spaces of the sky.
Be with them as they take to air,
In morning light and sunshine fair.

Eternal Father, strong to save,
Give them courage, make them brave;
Protect them whereso'er they go,
From shell and flak and fire and foe.

Most loved Member of their crew,
Ride with them up in the blue.
Direct their bombs upon the foe,
but shelter those whom Thou dost know.

Keep them together upon their way.
Grant their work success today.
Deliver them from hate and sin,
and bring them safely down again.

O God bless the men and women who fly,
Through lonely ways beneath the sky,

Amen

30 Day Prayer Challenge

Prayer is the Native Language of Faith.

Prayer list

What I'm Grateful For...

FAVORITE SCRIPTURES & QUOTES

MY NOTES

THOUGHTS & NOTES

Answered Prayers

30 Day Prayer Challenge

Prayer is the Native Language of Faith.

Prayer list

What I'm Grateful For...

FAVORITE SCRIPTURES & QUOTES

MY NOTES

THOUGHTS & NOTES

Answered Prayers

30 Day Prayer Challenge

Prayer is the Native Language of Faith.

Prayer list

What I'm Grateful For...

FAVORITE SCRIPTURES & QUOTES

MY NOTES

THOUGHTS & NOTES

Answered Prayers

30 Day Prayer Challenge

Prayer is the Native Language of Faith.

Prayer list

What I'm Grateful For...

FAVORITE SCRIPTURES & QUOTES

MY NOTES

THOUGHTS & NOTES

Answered Prayers

30 Day Prayer Challenge

Prayer is the Native Language of Faith.

Prayer list

What I'm Grateful For...

FAVORITE SCRIPTURES & QUOTES

MY NOTES

THOUGHTS & NOTES

Answered Prayers

30 Day Prayer Challenge

Prayer is the Native Language of Faith.

Prayer list

What I'm Grateful For...

FAVORITE SCRIPTURES & QUOTES

MY NOTES

THOUGHTS & NOTES

Answered Prayers

30 Day Prayer Challenge

Prayer is the Native Language of Faith.

Prayer list

What I'm Grateful For...

FAVORITE SCRIPTURES & QUOTES

MY NOTES

THOUGHTS & NOTES

Answered Prayers

30 Day Prayer Challenge

Prayer is the Native Language of Faith.

Prayer list

What I'm Grateful For...

FAVORITE SCRIPTURES & QUOTES

MY NOTES

THOUGHTS & NOTES

Answered Prayers

30 Day Prayer Challenge

Prayer is the Native Language of Faith.

Prayer list

What I'm Grateful For...

FAVORITE SCRIPTURES & QUOTES

MY NOTES

THOUGHTS & NOTES

Answered Prayers

30 Day Prayer Challenge

Prayer is the Native Language of Faith.

Prayer list

What I'm Grateful For...

FAVORITE SCRIPTURES & QUOTES

MY NOTES

THOUGHTS & NOTES

Answered Prayers

30 Day Prayer Challenge

Prayer is the Native Language of Faith.

Prayer list

What I'm Grateful For...

FAVORITE SCRIPTURES & QUOTES

MY NOTES

THOUGHTS & NOTES

Answered Prayers

30 Day Prayer Challenge

Prayer is the Native Language of Faith.

Prayer list

What I'm Grateful For...

FAVORITE SCRIPTURES & QUOTES

MY NOTES

THOUGHTS & NOTES

Answered Prayers

Made in the USA
Monee, IL
27 February 2022